MUSICIANS INSTITUTE

PRIVATE LESSONS

The Bassist's Guide to Time, Feel & Rhythm

by Oneida James

ISBN 0-634-06120-8

7777 W. BLUEMOUND RD. P.O. BOX 13819 MILWAUKEE, WI 53213

Visit Hal Leonard Online at
www.halleonard.com

In Australia Contact:
Hal Leonard Australia Pty. Ltd.
4 Lentara Court
Cheltenham, Victoria, 3192 Australia
Email: ausadmin@halleonard.com

Contents

Acknowledgments

This book is dedicated to my family.

Special thanks to Margaret A. Starks for National Teaching Standards consultation.

Introduction

The groove. It's the most important part of playing, and every successful rhythm musician has to have a handle on it. Surprisingly, many students of the bass completely overlook grooving and instead pursue less important aspects such as soloing, playing licks, slapping, etc., only to learn that they need to back-track and seriously spend time on their groove. While the other aspects of playing are very important, a tremendous amount of time and study should be dedicated to grooving, especially for a foundation instrument such as the bass guitar.

The concepts in this book were developed over many years of live playing, recording, and teaching live playing workshops and private lessons. Often, my students were from foreign countries and presented a language barrier, making it even more difficult to communicate the abstract concepts involved in grooving. This made it necessary for me to 1) be very thoughtful in developing a method, and 2) communicate this method in a very clear, direct, and understandable way. I have isolated a series of topics along with their attendant problems and practice remedies, which, when applied with serious dedication, will truly enhance and improve a player's groove.

Please note that this book is for players of intermediate level and higher. It is not for beginners, as you'll need some level of proficiency to get the desired results. In addition, this book should be used in conjunction with bass technique and music theory studies, as groove is a separate and more abstract part of overall musicianship.

About the Groove Mastery CD

The Groove Mastery CD included with this book contains audio performances of all the written exercises referenced in the coming chapters. Audio icons with track numbers are given at the beginning of each exercise. Each exercise/groove has 2 tracks, one with the bass line recorded and the other without the bass line recorded so you can play along.

Getting the Best Results from This Book

It's important to monitor your own progress while working on the concepts presented in this book. This means recording and listening to your playing on a regular basis, keeping a written practice schedule, logging time spent, materials covered, achievements reached, and problems to be fixed.

Always practice with a metronome, at different tempos and in all positions up and down the neck of the bass. This will be discussed in more detail in the chapters on techniques and practicing.

It is very important that you have a good music listening system, for use with this book, and for listening and transcribing in general. Consider it a part of your gear. You'll want to make sure you're not missing important nuances of the bass performances that you are transcribing. Using earphones is always a good way to hear what you need to hear.

Once you feel comfortable with an exercise or groove, record yourself playing with a metronome and listen back to your performance. When recording yourself for the purpose of perfecting your groove, a metronome is preferable to a drum machine because while the drum machine is easier to play along with, the metronome will give a brutally stark representation of your own sense of time—a very important part of the learning process. At times, however, some of the exercises/grooves will call for a drum machine, as it is also a very useful tool. Another great way to visually assess your timing is to record yourself with a computer-based recording program such as Digital Performer, ProTools, Cakewalk, Digital Orchestrator, etc. In addition to accurately recording your playing, these software programs provide a graphical representation of the sound waves produced by your instrument. When using them, you can actually see where your notes start and end in relation to the metronome. This technique of recording and listening back will be a theme throughout this book.

The chapters in this book are for the most part self-contained, so if you find that you would like to take them in a different order, feel free to do so. However, some topics overlap and cross-reference each other, so it's not a good idea to ignore any chapter entirely. As you make your way through the book you will notice that some chapters are more difficult than others. It is a good idea to note those chapters and continue to work with them after you have finished the book.

Lastly, my website, www.groovemastery.com, will serve as an extension of this book. When you visit, you will find additional grooves, exercises, tips, and resources to aid in your journey to groove mastery. Other services include personal groove analysis, lessons, and one-on-one guidance working through this book.

Below is a list of tools which will be necessary in the use of the book. I recommend that you have these at your disposal to start this process.

Tools:
- Metronome
- Drum machine
- Earphones
- CD player
- Groove Mastery CD included with this book
- Digital recorder, minidisc, or cassette recorder

If you have a computer:
- Legal internet music download site
- Recording software such as ProTools or Sonar

Note to Educators

This book addresses the following National Learning Standards for music.

NA.9-12.2 PERFORMING ON INSTRUMENTS, ALONE AND WITH OTHERS, A VARIED REPERTOIRE OF MUSIC

Achievement Standard, Proficient:
- Students perform with expression and technical accuracy a large and varied repertoire of instrumental literature with a level of difficulty of 4, on a scale of 1 to 6
- Students perform an appropriate part in an ensemble, demonstrating well-developed ensemble skills
- Students perform in small ensembles with one student on a part

Achievement Standard, Advanced:
- Students perform with expression and technical accuracy a large and varied repertoire of instrumental literature with a level of difficulty of 5, on a scale of 1 to 6

NA.9-12.6 LISTENING TO, ANALYZING, AND DESCRIBING MUSIC

Achievement Standard, Proficient:
- Students analyze aural examples of a varied repertoire of music, representing diverse genres and cultures, by describing the uses of elements of music and expressive devices
- Students demonstrate extensive knowledge of the technical vocabulary of music
- Students identify and explain compositional devices and techniques used to provide unity and variety and tension and release in a musical work and give examples of other works that make similar uses of these devices and techniques

Achievement Standard, Advanced:
- Students demonstrate the ability to perceive and remember music events by describing in detail significant events (e.g., fugal entrances, chromatic modulations, developmental devices) occurring in a given aural example
- Students compare ways in which musical materials are used in a given example relative to ways in which they are used in other works of the same genre or style
- Students analyze and describe uses of the elements of music in a given work that make it unique, interesting, and expressive

NA.9-12.7 EVALUATING MUSIC AND MUSIC PERFORMANCES

Achievement Standard, Proficient:
- Students evolve specific criteria for making informed, critical evaluations of the quality and effectiveness of performances, compositions, arrangements, and improvisations, and apply the criteria in their personal participation in music
- Students evaluate a performance, composition, arrangement, or improvisation by comparing it to similar or exemplary models

Achievement Standard, Advanced:
- Students evaluate a given musical work in terms of its aesthetic qualities and explain the musical means it uses to evoke feelings and emotions

Developing Your Feel for Time

1

Defining Groove

Groove is your most passionate expression of feeling time through playing your instrument.

What is being "in the groove?" Though each rhythm instrument has its own job to perform, when all are in the groove, they sound and feel like one instrument. It's that place where every note and every lick of every instrument fit just perfectly in a musical performance. It depends on the ability of each musician to be a team player and create the best feel for that particular piece of music.

Think about the vinyl recordings that hip-hop DJs use. When you set the stylus on the vinyl, it settles perfectly into the groove of that vinyl recording in order to play the contents. The only way the contents of the vinyl will be heard is if the stylus sits perfectly in this groove. If the arm holding the stylus is too light, it will skip all the way across the disk and the music will not play. If the arm is too heavy or the stylus is misshapen, it will damage the vinyl record. There has to be a perfect balance and fit to create the desired result.

Think of your playing as the stylus and the music you are to perform as the vinyl record. When your playing fits perfectly into the music, consider yourself "in the groove."

You will want to develop your instincts for playing notes in the most comfortable sounding, best feeling place within a musical phrase or bass line. This place is often referred to as the "pocket." This is an abstract concept that can be difficult to grasp. However, when given a roadmap and techniques for dissecting one's playing, the objective of playing consistently "in the pocket" can always be achieved with dedication and hard work.

Upbeat/Downbeat Combinations

To begin the process of developing your feel for time, we will start with standard 4/4 quarter notes subdivided into sixteenth notes. If you are familiar with the concepts of subdivision and syncopation, feel free to skip over the following explanation. Continue reading at the bottom paragraph.

Below is one measure of four quarter notes. Each quarter note gets one beat. If you tap your foot while playing, it should tap four times for the example. When each quarter note is evenly subdivided into four smaller notes, they are called sixteenths. While tapping the foot **only** in quarter notes, we count each sixteenth note aloud: "**one** e and a, **two** e and a, **three** e and a, **four** e and a."

Quarter Note Subdivisions

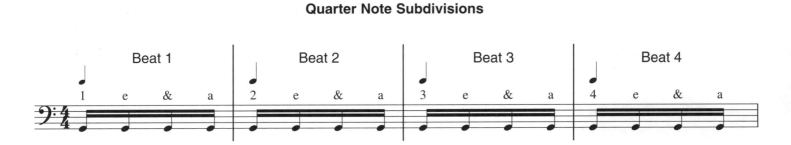

For each beat, then, there are four sixteenth notes, each with its own name. In addition to this, each sixteenth note is categorized as either a **downbeat** or an **upbeat**. The first sixteenth ("one") is called a downbeat, the second sixteenth ("e") is called an upbeat, the third sixteenth ("and") is called a downbeat, and the fourth sixteenth ("a") is called an upbeat.

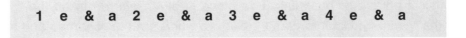

Notice that while the "and" of each beat is referred to as a downbeat, it does not mean you should put your foot down here. Tap the foot only on the numbers. Your foot should reach its highest point exactly on the "and."

Rhythms using certain combinations of "e" and "a" upbeats with downbeats create **syncopation**, or accents on unexpected beats, which can be very difficult to play. Hip-hop, R&B, reggae, funk, contemporary jazz, and even some pop music styles are based on grooves which contain intricate syncopation, so understanding and being able to play syncopated rhythms is essential. First we will learn the basics of playing them. Then, we'll work on playing them "in the groove" a little later.

Following are exercises that offer some challenging upbeat/downbeat combinations. However, you'll find that these exercises are not technically challenging. Listen to each exercise on the CD, familiarize yourself with the rhythms, and play each along with a metronome, away from the CD. The ones that are more difficult will let you know which areas need work. For instance, if you notice any of these:

- The first beat of the phrase is rushed or played inconsistently.
- You cannot play the syncopated pattern.
- You drag the upbeat note to the next downbeat.
- You are guessing at the rhythm.

Slow the metronome down, count the example aloud until you are sure you know upon which beat every note falls, and then use the process of recording and listening until you can play the phrase consistently every time. Do not increase the tempo until you can perform the pattern consistently. Then move the tempo up a little at a time until you surpass the original tempo by fifteen bpm. By doing this, you ensure that you can perform the upbeat/downbeat combinations at any tempo, thereby strengthening your feel and ability to play syncopated figures in time. Listen very carefully to your recorded performances—only your best is good enough for the groove.

Syncopation Exercise 1

Perform this exercise as follows:

1. Listen to Track 1 and memorize the bass line (the written notation is only a guide). Play it with a metronome at a slow enough tempo so that you can count it accurately, and then work up the tempo as described above. Only when it is comfortable with the metronome should you play with the recording.
2. Play with the recording several times.
3. Finally, record yourself playing with Track 2.

When you listen back to your performance, compare it to Track 1, with the recorded bass line. Check for consistency: that the line is played the same, without changing the syncopation or rushing the upbeats. There are of course other things to check and we will get into those things later in the book. At this stage, the important thing is that you play this line with the correct syncopation. The first two beats of bars 1 and 3 are the problematic parts of this bass line as far as syncopation is concerned. If you find it difficult to play these, loop the two beats and play them at approximately 85 bpm until the passage becomes easy to play.

When (not before) you can perform this groove with ease at the recommended tempo and up to fifteen bpm faster, then move to the next groove.

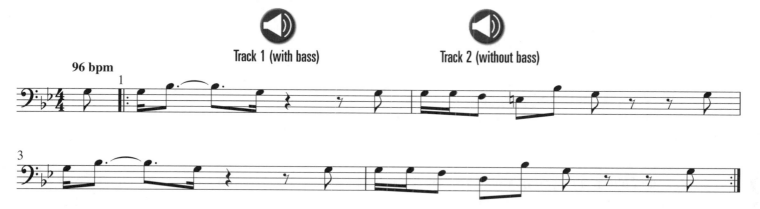

Track 1 (with bass)   Track 2 (without bass)

96 bpm

Syncopation Exercise 2

This exercise emphasizes each of the sixteenth-note subdivisions within a quarter note. Review the sub-divisions ("one e and a, two e and a, three e and a, four e and a") at the beginning of this chapter, if needed.

Here is a breakdown of what we're about to play:
- The first quarter beat has a note on the "one" sixteenth subdivision.
- The second quarter beat has a note on the "e" sixteenth subdivision.
- The third quarter beat has a note on the "and" sixteenth subdivision.
- The fourth quarter beat has a note on the "a" sixteenth subdivision.

Part B of the exercise contains the same attacks, but in the key of G, with an additional sixteenth note added after each. Part B starts at 1:47 in Track 3.

Track 3 (with bass)   Track 4 (without bass)

After memorizing and practicing with a metronome and Track 3, record yourself playing with Track 4.

My experience with this exercise is that whenever a student finds a syncopated rhythm to be difficult, the tendency is to guess at it, with the result being an inconsistent groove that sounds hesitant and unsure. If, however, the exact subdivided rhythm is understood and internalized before playing, you won't have to guess, you'll be able to nail it.

If you have difficulty playing Syncopation Exercise 2, break it up into four one-beat exercises, each con-taining one beat's worth of the original example. Count each sixteenth note aloud ("one e and a") and play the note on the correct subdivision.

Here's a description of the process. Set your metronome to play sixteenths at 70 bpm (slow the tempo further if necessary). Take one quarter note measurement at a time and loop it, while continuing to count "one e and a" aloud.

Beat One				
Sing:	one	e	and	a
Play:	A	rest	rest	rest
Beat Two				
Sing:	two	e	and	a
Play:	rest	C♯	rest	rest
Beat Three				
Sing:	three	e	and	a
Play:	rest	rest	D	rest
Beat Four				
Sing:	4	e	and	a
Play:	rest	rest	rest	E

Loop each pattern until you can play it easily. Then try increasing the tempo a few bpm at a time, up to 120. Then start putting the pieces back together, two beats, three beats, then finally the whole measure.

Syncopation Exercise 3

The rhythm of the first two beats in measure 1 form the basis for the rest of this groove. To practice it a little at a time, isolate the first two beats by adding a half rest to make one whole measure. Then loop that pattern at the slower tempo of 85 bpm. Memorize the rhythm of the first two beats and note how often it repeats in this four-measure pattern. This will help you to understand this syncopation combination. For measure 4, loop the second two beats, this time adding a half rest to the beginning of the phrase to make one whole measure.

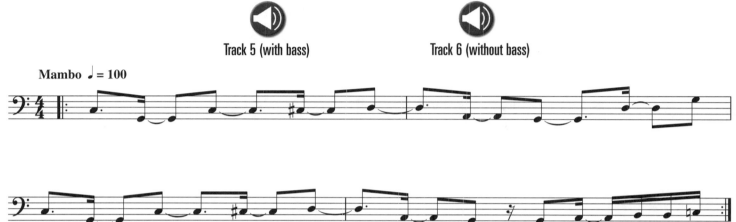

Track 5 (with bass)   Track 6 (without bass)

Mambo ♩ = 100

Don't fret if you can't nail these exercises right away. Simply make a note to practice them every day until you can perform them easily at slower and faster tempos. With time you'll have a confident grasp of syncopation.

Note Placement

Now that you've worked on some syncopated exercises, it's time to look at playing them "in the groove" by analyzing your exact note placement. This will let you begin to measure how well you groove.

In regard to feel for time, note placement refers to exactly when your notes are landing in relation to any metronomic upbeat or downbeat. The notes you play may generally fall:

a) slightly before the beat. The common terms for playing before the beat are **rushing**, playing **in front** of, or **on top** of the beat. This is still considered to be "in time" with the music but can cause a tense, rushed, or pushed feel.

b) right on the beat. This is a good thing for certain kinds of music such as rock, disco, and other dance music with tempos of 115 and higher, but it can cause a "sequenced" or machine-like feel in other situations.

c) slightly (very slightly) behind the beat. This can create a very relaxed "pocket."

d) even more behind the beat (still in time but can make for a dragging, loose, or "flamming" sound).

Note Placement Exercise 1

The following examples use sound wave imagery for two measures of quarter notes so you can see how moving notes in small increments looks and sounds, to help visualize the concept of note placement (playing in front, behind, etc.). The notes you see below are from the exact recordings used in the grooves on the CD.

Listen closely to Tracks 7–10, with the bass playing in front, right on, slightly behind, and far behind the beat. As you listen to the grooves, note the feeling each way of playing creates.

Track 7

In Front

In this visual note placement example, the notes land before the downbeats.

Track 8

Right On

In this note placement example, the note lands right on the downbeat.

Chapter 1

Slightly Behind

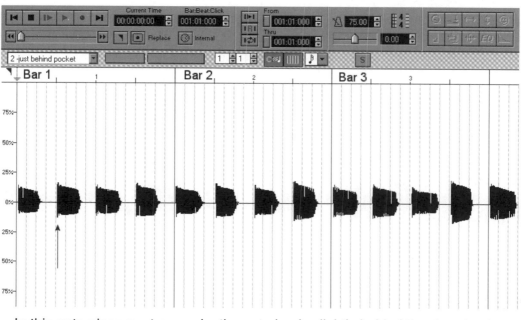

In this note placement example, the note lands slightly behind the downbeat.

Far Behind

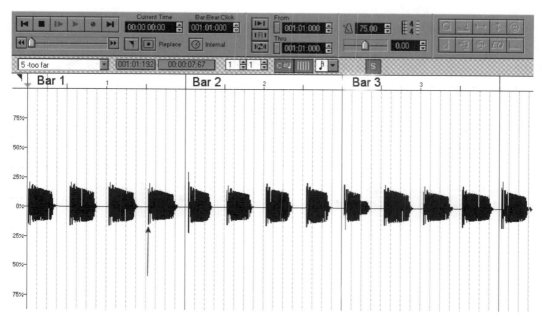

In this note placement example, the note lands too far behind the downbeat.

Use Track 11 to practice playing quarter notes as in Note Placement Exercise 1: in front, right on, slightly behind, then far behind the beat. Record your playing, and then listen closely to see if you successfully created the four feels.

Note Placement Exercise 2

This exercise is divided into four parts, one for each of the four feels we explored in Note Placement Exercise 1. Pick a groove that you are familiar with playing (use a metronome in this case). Choose one that has a moderate degree of difficulty with syncopation. If you don't have one you can use Syncopation Exercise 1 (Track 2). Record yourself playing along with the groove as follows:

1. Record yourself playing slightly in front of the beat. Before going on to the next part, record and listen back to your performance several times. Listen for consistency: that all of your notes (and thus your performance) are on top or in front of the beat, not all over the place. Once you are satisfied that your performance is consistent, use this process for Parts Two, Three, and Four of the exercise.

2. Play and record right on the beat.

3. Play and record slightly behind the beat.

4. Play and record far behind the beat.

Remember not to go to the next part until you feel your performances are consistent. Take your time with this exercise and go back to it frequently, substituting other grooves. As you master each of these in your practice, you can begin to take the skills into live playing situations.

Practice listening very closely until you can hear the difference between these examples. Hearing small increments such as these is a developed skill which may be difficult at first. But the more you work with note placement, in listening to yourself and other instruments and players, the stronger this skill will become, making it easier to hear these small time increments and how they contribute to, or detract from, the groove.

One of the most important things to remember in note placement is that all of the above examples may or may not be desirable in a given song. In both live and recording situations, there will be times when you are called upon to lay your groove way back, push it forward, etc. The better you understand "feel for time" and the more experience you have with this concept, the easier it will be for you to make such adjustments in your playing.

Laying Back

2

"Lay back!" is probably the most common expression that my fellow teachers and I have uttered over the years of live-playing workshops. For most students, laying back is one of the biggest hurdles they face, even if they have other aspects of their playing under control. It seems that even though one is aware of the need to lay back, this skill doesn't just come by the knowledge that it needs to be there.

I think of laying back as relaxing the groove; feeling the space between the notes; making the groove sound easy. It's the ability to manipulate very small increments of time, once you've developed the instincts to know when it is necessary to do so. Don't confuse laying back with dragging, there's a big difference. Laying back is sinking back just into the "pocket," while dragging is sinking too far back into a slower tempo.

A laid-back groove is a much-coveted thing among musicians, because once you can control laying back (or pushing forward, or anywhere in between), you will genuinely have a great feel for time. This is the mark of a mature, seasoned player. "Pushing" the groove forward can be just as valuable a skill as laying it back, when it is called for by the music.

Usually, there is so much to absorb as a beginning student of the bass that laying back can be viewed as a concept that is way too abstract to include in early study. Students don't usually start thinking in these terms until much later in the process of learning. It takes time to become a good musician and even longer to become a seasoned groover, but if you are aware of all of the issues involved in laying back, feel for time, grooving, etc., and incorporate them into your study early on, you will reach your goals much sooner.

Five Stages of Awareness

There are generally five stages of awareness that students go through when they begin to work on their grooves.

1. Stage one is the "What are you talking about?—I don't hear myself rushing/dragging/playing uneven notes/phrasing inconsistently" stage. You are able to be musical and therefore, play and hear with some level of proficiency. However, your ear is not yet developed enough to hear the small time intervals required to lay back or push your groove, among other things. Don't worry, once you are attuned, developing an ear for hearing the small increments will happen.

2. Stage two is the "What the heck is my problem?" stage. You will be able to hear yourself rushing or dragging, but you won't be able to place the notes where you want to place them with any consistency.

3. Stage three is the "I think I'm getting the hang of this—I can do this, but something's not quite right" stage. You will begin to place notes where you want them except for difficult subdivision combinations.

4. Stage four is when you think, "I'm really excited, I've almost got this thing under control." You will be able to place notes where you want them consistently, including difficult subdivision combinations. However, tense playing situations like auditions, live gigs, and recording sessions will distract you, causing you to revert to old habits.

5. Stage five is the "NOW I get it!" stage! You will be able to place notes where you want them consistently, even in stressful situations. When you have reached this level, you are in good shape—you're a seasoned groover.

Those who don't take an active role in working on their playing run the risk of getting stuck at one of these stages. The longer they continue with bad habits, the more difficult they will be to correct once they are addressed. There is a definite line that one crosses from being "someone who plays the bass" to a seasoned groover; there's a time when people hear you play and say, "Wow, how long have you been playing, your groove is great." But that doesn't happen until after you have done the work.

Identify where you are in these five stages, so you can mark your growth and feel great about it as you move along.

Building Your Foundation

3

There are many elements to building your foundation, and it will require lots of time and effort on your part. This is one of the biggest investments you can make towards having a great groove.

Studying Other Bass Players

Notice I used the word "studying" as opposed to "listening to" other bass players. I believe it's important to look at the body of these players' (and innovators') work. You will gain valuable information and skills, such as the stylistic elements of different genres, and how a particular player influenced not only bass playing, but the style and sound of the music. This in turn gives you the tools you will need to contribute your creativity in live and/or recording situations. For instance, in studying the late great James Jamerson (whom, by the way, I believe every bass player should study), I learned how to outline and color chord changes in the context of playing mainstream music, as this is one of the timeless elements of his playing.

A very important part of studying other players is building your Bassist's Reference List. Not only should you listen to and study the songs and players on this list, but you should transcribe each bass line note-for-note. A crucial benefit of building and working with your list is that you are expanding your vocabulary. That is, you are creating your own arsenal of licks, grooves, techniques, styles, etc. from which you can draw. These are references that add depth, dimension of color, and maturity to your playing. The fuller your list of references, the richer your playing will be.

Perhaps most importantly, this process will help to develop your ear. Your hearing is obviously the most valuable tool you have, and it needs to be worked on in the same way that muscles need exercise and strength building to become stronger. Often, my students ask for charts to aid them in live playing workshops and groove master classes. Even when charts are available, I will ask the students to use their ears and transcribe the songs themselves. In the real world of auditioning, performing, and recording, charts are not handed out most of the time.

Following is a partial list of bass players who have been pioneers and innovators of funk, rock, R&B, and pop, and who have blessed us with their talent, creativity, and innovation. Many of the songs/albums are from classic genres. I have also included some classic songs/albums on which these players have performed and/or artists they have worked with in live performance. The well-rounded bassist must study the classics. Use this as a place to start and build on to it to make the list your own, creating a library of songs for transcribing, studying, and listening.

You will notice the list is weighted toward the R&B and funk areas. This is a deliberate action because though most contemporary music requires a strong groove, R&B and funk are the quintessential groove genres.

To use this chart, and as part of building your lists, you will need an effective way to find the music. I have found that using a legal download site is the most efficient way to collect material.

Bassist's Reference List

BASSIST	SONG/ARTIST/ALBUM	GENRE
James Jamerson	"My Girl"–Temptations "Bernadette"–Four Tops "Ain't That Peculiar"–Marvin Gaye "Ooh Baby Baby"–The Miracles "I Heard It Through the Grapevine" (2 recordings)–Marvin Gaye, Gladys Knight and the Pips "Love Child"–Diana Ross and the Supremes "What's Going On"–Marvin Gaye "You Keep Me Hanging On"–Diana/Supremes "Ain't No Mountain High Enough"–Marvin Gaye/Tammy Terrell, Diana/Supremes "Signed, Sealed, Delivered"–Stevie Wonder	Classic R&B
Marcus Miller	Produced albums by such renowned performers as Miles Davis, David Sanborn, Luther Vandross, Al Jarreau, The Crusaders and, as bassist, has appeared and/or recorded with Miles Davis, David Sanborn, Luther Vandross, Joe Sample, McCoy Tyner and Jackie McLean, Grover Washington, Jr., Aretha Franklin, Roberta Flack, Never Too Much, Tu Tu	Jazz, Contemporary Jazz, Pop, Rock, Contemporary R&B, R&B Funk
Anthony Jackson	Chaka Khan, Chick Corea, Michel Camilo, Steve Khan, Steely Dan, The O'Jays, Roberta Flack, Dave Grusin, Buddy Rich, Horace Silver, Al DiMeola, Paul Simon	Contemporary R&B
Neil Stubenhaus	Michael Bolton, David Benoit, Luis Miguel, Bobby Caldwell, Neil Diamond, Cher, Natalie Cole, Dan Hill, Quincy Jones, Patti LaBelle, Wilson Phillips, Julio Iglesias, The Manhattan Transfer, Bette Midler, Tom Scott, Barbra Streisand, Lalah Hathaway	
Nathan East	Anita Baker, Eric Clapton, Elton John, Michael Jackson, Whitney Houston, Babyface, Quincy Jones, Al Jarreau, David Benoit. Co-wrote the #1 hit song "Easy Lover" with Phil Collins and Philip Bailey	
Flea	Red Hot Chili Peppers	Alternative, Funk Rock, Rock, Pop

BASSIST	SONG/ARTIST/ALBUM	GENRE
Darryl Jones	Sting–*Bring on the Night*, Rolling Stones–*No Security, Bridges to Babylon, Out of Control in Chicago, Secret Service*, Joe Cocker–*Organic*, Joan Armatrading–*What's Inside*, Miles Davis–*You're Under Arrest, Decoy, Human Nature*, Phillip Bailey–*Inside Out*, Randy Brecker–*Toe to Toe*	Rock, Pop, R&B, Contemporary Jazz
Louis Johnson	Brothers Johnson, Michael Jackson, George Benson, Aretha Franklin, Herbie Hancock, Herb Alpert, Chaka Kahn, Donna Summer, Bobby Womack, and many of Quincy Jones's LPs	Classic R&B, Contemporary R&B
Chuck Rainey	Steely Dan–*Gaucho, Aja, The Royal Scam, Katy Lied, Pretzel Logic*, Marvin Gaye–*I Want You*, Quincy Jones	Contemporary Jazz, Classic R&B
Lee Sklar	James Taylor, Linda Ronstadt, Hall and Oates, Phil Collins, Reba McEntire, George Strait	Pop, Soft Rock, Classic Rock
Will Lee	*The Late Show with David Letterman*, Mariah Carey, Ricky Martin, D'Angelo, Carly Simon, Steely Dan, Cat Stevens, Michael Bolton, Ringo Starr, Laura Nyro, Spyro Gyra, Gloria Estefan and the Miami Sound Machine, Nancy Wilson, Luther Vandross, Cyndi Lauper, Chaka Khan, James Brown, George Benson, Bette Midler, Barry Manilow, Cher, Michael Franks, Weather Report, Al Green, the Brecker Brothers, Frank Sinatra, Barbra Streisand, Diana Ross, David Sanborn, Natalie Cole, Gato Barbieri	Pop, Contemporary R&B, Live playing
Willie Weeks	Donny Hathaway	Classic R&B
Rocco Prestia	Tower of Power	Funk/R&B/Pop
Larry Graham	Sly and the Family Stone, Graham Central Station, Prince	Classic R&B, Funk, Funk Rock
Andrew Gushea	The Winans	Contemporary Gospel, Contemporary R&B

Study Questions

Every bass groove has certain elements that make it work. The following list of questions is designed to help you analyze what a player does to make a groove work (or not). Ask and answer these as you study the recorded works or live performances of any player. Add more questions to it and make it your own.

- What do you think was the most important part of the bass line?
- What do you think makes the bass line groove?
- What are the strong beats/notes (most important or emphasized)?
- Did this player use mostly sixteenth notes? Quarter notes? Eighth notes?
- Did this player outline chords in a colorful way by playing 3rds, 4ths, 6ths, 7ths, and 10ths, or did this player use a minimalist approach, sticking to roots, 5ths, and octaves?
- Did this player follow the kick drum pattern?
- Do you recognize the playing style of this player when you hear other recordings? Why?
- Do you recognize this player's influences?
- Do you ever hear other players emulating this bass player?
- What type of music did this player perform?
- What are some of the differences in the playing style of this player vs. another of your favorite players?
- Did this player play signature or memorable licks? Have you transcribed and used any of these licks?
- Are there any elements of this player's style that you can use?
- Did this player use the slap technique? Do you recognize the characteristics of this slap technique?
- Did this player use chords, glissando, harmonics, double stops, etc. in his/her recordings?
- How would you sum up this player's style? Funky, technical, mature, melodic? Heavy on the chops, etc.?

You should continue this type of study not only as a new student of the bass, but throughout your career. If you wish to continue to grow as a player, there is always an ever-growing wealth of talent from which draw.

Players who don't study other bassists in order to broaden their repertoire tend to sound shallow, without a developed style or sound. I'm sure you've heard players who sound this way. When you practice or play only what you already know or only what is in your head, the process of growing as a player is stifled. Another common mistake is to listen to and study only one bass player. The problem here is that you run the risk of sounding too much like that particular player, which can make your sound one-dimensional and does not allow for an appropriate flow from one genre to the next. If you are striving to be a well-rounded player, obviously this will cause many problems. So, don't get stuck listening to only one style of music, and don't get stuck listening to only one bass player.

The process of studying other bass players gives these and other benefits.
- Aids in learning to groove
- Builds chops
- Provides inspiration
- Helps you develop your own style and sound
- Creates the desire to stretch in your creativity and musicianship
- Fill in your thoughts _____
  _____
  _____

Genres

In case it's not clear, for the purpose of musical study, genre and style are not quite the same thing. A **genre** is an overall category of music, whereas **style** is a particular manner in which music is performed. Thus we can say that a particular R&B bassist (who specializes in the R&B genre) has a style (way of performing it) that is: aggressive, mellow, primitive, sophisticated, funky, etc.

Not only do genres of music today have roots in those of yesterday, concurrent ones also borrow elements from each other. For instance, some elements of pop are infused with contemporary R&B or hip-hop in the music of Junior/Senior and Justin Timberlake. Some genres of alternative and rock may have elements of funk, i.e., Kid Rock, Lenny Kravitz, G-Love, and The Red Hot Chili Peppers. It is important to have at least a basic knowledge of many genres. In order to play contemporary R&B or hip-hop competently, one must have ample references from the funk and classic R&B genres. And likewise, in order to be a competent player in some styles of hard rock, knowledge of classic rock is necessary.

On the other hand, it's a bad idea to mix elements of different genres in the same song at random and without forethought. Your basic mission statement regarding genre is to know what is called for and how to play it. You need an arsenal of styles, references, licks, and chops for every genre if you want to increase your chances for success as a bassist.

Listening/Analysis Exercise

This is a series of grooves given to demonstrate the general style and characteristics of bass playing for a particular genre. Give some time and thought to the differences, similarities, whys, and hows of the grooves. The goal is to recognize and generate these characteristics in your own playing.

For this exercise, you will:
1. Listen to and learn the grooves. There are (intentionally) no charts given for the grooves so you will be using your ears.
2. Analyze each groove's characteristics and write down your observations.

First we have a "Blurry," Puddle of Mudd-type alternative groove. I'll start you off by making the first analysis (feel free to add more observations of your own):

Track 12 (with bass)

Track 13 (without bass)

Song	Genre	Characteristic 1	Char. 2	Char. 3	Char. 4	Char. 5
In the style of "Blurry"	Alternative rock	Bass line follows kick drum	Entire groove is legato	Colorful, (adding 3rds, 4ths, 6ths, 7ths) playing through chord changes	No ghost notes	Lots of movement from dotted 8th-16th feel to 16th notes, especially toward the end of performance

Now it's your turn to analyze the next bass groove. Track 13 is a contemporary R&B-type groove in the style of D'Angelo.

Track 14 (with bass)   Track 15 (without bass)

Song	Genre	Characteristic 1	Char. 2	Char. 3	Char. 4	Char. 5

Now change to Track 16 for our next example. It's a Jackson Five "I Want You Back" classic R&B-type groove.

Track 16 (with bass)   Track 17 (without bass)

Song	Genre	Characteristic 1	Char. 2	Char. 3	Char. 4	Char. 5

Our next example is a Parliament/Funkadelic-type funk groove.

Track 18 (with bass)   Track 19 (without bass)

Song	Genre	Characteristic 1	Char. 2	Char. 3	Char. 4	Char. 5

Track 20 is a Neo Soul-type groove.

Track 20 (with bass)

Track 21 (without bass)

Song	Genre	Characteristic 1	Char. 2	Char. 3	Char. 4	Char. 5

Finally, we have a classic rock groove in the style of "Walk This Way" by Aerosmith.

Track 22 (with bass)

Track 23 (without bass)

Song	Genre	Characteristic 1	Char. 2	Char. 3	Char. 4	Char. 5

Be thorough in your analysis, as this will help to open your creative thought process in the studio and live performances. Bass lines often cross genres, and often, crossing genres creates new sub-genres. The more knowledgeable you are about the characteristics of playing in these genres, the better you will be able to maneuver between them while contributing your own creativity.

Listening

4

Any musician who wants to achieve a professional playing level knows he/she must practice often and consistently. What many players miss is the importance of listening as part of practicing. One reason it's so important is this: after you have digested all of the technical aspects of playing, you must make the connection between intellect (playing from your head) and feeling (playing from your heart). In the process of listening long enough to many styles, players, and genres (along with consistent practice), you begin to internally make this connection. Once this head-heart connection is made internally, you can then bring it out through your instrument. When you begin to master this, you begin to master groove.

I've noticed four major listening-related roadblocks that hampered the majority of my students. Each has a listening-based remedy that I usually prescribe.

1. Listen First, Play Later

The first roadblock is that in attempting to transcribe bass lines, students incorrectly interpret them and/or leave out important elements or nuances. The remedy for this is to first study the music *without* your instrument in your hands.

This part of listening especially applies to learning new material. If you need to learn material for a rehearsal, audition, performance, etc., listen to the entire piece of music two or three times before you even pick up your instrument to play. Without the distraction of the instrument you will be better able to discern:

- The form of the song.
- The length of band phrases: one, two, four, or eight bars, etc.
- The length of bass notes.
- Important licks and when they should occur.
- How the bass line should really sound when played correctly.

If, on the other hand, you begin playing along as soon as you hear the piece of music, you run the risk of not picking up enough of the important elements of the bass line, such as how it fits in the overall picture, or what gives the line its character and vibe, all of which you must be able to reproduce for a good groove.

2. Commit to Long-Term Listening

The second roadblock to grooving is basic unfamiliarity with genres and styles. I've had many students who've wanted to learn how to play contemporary or classic R&B, hip-hop, alternative, reggae, or other styles, while never having listened to much of any of them. When they attempt to play this music, the truth comes out: they sound as though they've never heard or played these styles. They simply don't have the references of the genre or the players who performed it, even though they may have all the technical aspects of playing the bass under control.

Here is what I mean by long-term listening:

- Make the ongoing commitment to listen to a wide variety of music as often as possible.
- Listen to music as much as possible.
- Listen to as many styles and genres as possible.
- Listen to as many players as possible.
- Listen as much as possible, in your car, at home, at work etc., etc.
- Create a library of music in all styles and genres and listen to these songs over and over.
- Every way you can imagine—listen till the music is a part of you!
- When you can't stand to listen anymore, then listen some more.

Be passionate about listening and growing the music inside you, and love it. There is no way to be able to play music from the heart if the music is not there to begin with. This is very important! Throughout my many years of teaching, when I asked students to whom and what they listen to, or what they want to learn to play, I consistently received responses such as: "Oh, I only listen to this player," or "Oh, I've never listened to anything but this style of music," or "I don't listen to anything but my own music." If your goal is to be a well-rounded player and a groover, this is NOT the way to go!

The professional player has mastered the art of slipping from one form of music to the next. This doesn't happen by itself. It's because of his or her foundation. If you're playing hard rock or contemporary R&B, you don't want to sound like a "light-hitting jazzer." If you're playing blues, you don't want to leave out the important elements of blues. If you've played and listened to nothing but rock, then your funk playing will probably be lacking in the elements of funk. I've heard of many players who have gotten fired for this reason, or who never got the gig they wanted because they "sounded too jazzy." Or, they got the gig with their impressive chops, only to lose it later when all the dazzle wore off and it became apparent they weren't contributing to the groove with the right stylistic elements for the situation.

Though a recorded bass line may sound easy, the bassist who performed it brought his/her fifteen, twenty, or more years of experience, style, and chops to the performance. Many of the players you are studying are amazing musicians with very strong roots in jazz. You are giving respect to the player when you apply long-term listening.

A must-see movie for students of the bass (and other rhythm instruments) is *Standing in the Shadows of Motown*. This movie demonstrates the amazing backgrounds, talents, creativity, and innovations of some of the musicians who created the mainstream pop, R&B, and funk sounds of the sixties and seventies. This music has been extremely influential in virtually every style of mainstream music today. As you study and give respect to these musicians by recognizing their musical choices and approaches, you reap the benefits of their contributions. It is a tribute to their talents that many of the elements of their playing are very valid today.

Below is a partial list of suggested music for long-term listening. There are some very excellent bass performances and lots to study. Continue to add to your list and make it your own. Though you may have your favorite type of music, your choices should still be varied.

Music Listening Chart

Song/Album	Artist	Bassist	Genre
What Cha' Gonna Do for Me, Naughty	Chaka Kahn	Anthony Jackson	Contemporary R&B
"For the Love of Money"	The O'Jays	Darryl Jones	Classic R&B
"Tell Me a Bedtime Story," "Along Came Betty"	Quincy Jones	Chuck Rainey	Contemporary Jazz
Aja	Steely Dan	Chuck Rainey	Pop/rock
"What's Goin' On?"	Marvin Gaye	James Jamerson	Classic R&B
"What's Goin' On?"	Donny Hathaway	Willie Weeks	Classic R&B
Waterfalls	TLC	Marq Jefferson	Contemporary R&B
Best of Rufus Featuring Chaka Khan	Rufus	Bobby Watson	R&B
Rhythm of Love	Anita Baker	Nathan East	Contemporary R&B
Different Lifestyles	BeBe and CeCe Winans	Andrew Gouche, Keith Thomas	Contemporary Gospel
What Hits, By the Way, Bass Signature Licks	The Red Hot Chili Peppers	Flea	Alternative
The Heart of a Man	Phil Perry	Neil Stubenhaus	Contemporary R&B
"Stay Home Tonight"	Lalah Hathaway	Neil Stubenhaus	Contemporary R&B
Compositions	Anita Baker	Nathan East	Contemporary Jazz
Best of the Yellowjackets	The Yellowjackets	Jimmy Haslip	Jazz Fusion

Song/Album	Artist	Bassist	Genre
Live and More, The Sun Don't Lie	Marcus Miller	Marcus Miller	Contemporary Jazz
The Best of Tower of Power	Tower of Power	Rocco Prestia	Funk
The Best of Brothers Johnson	Brothers Johnson	Louis Johnson	Funk/Classic R&B
"Men In Black II Theme"	Various Artists	Darryl Jones	Urban/Funk
Best of Larry Graham	Larry Graham	Larry Graham	Funk
D'Angelo	Brown Sugar	Will Lee, Larry Grenadier	Urban/R&B/Hip Hop
"Lay Your Troubles Down"	Angela Winbush	Nathan East	Contemporary R&B
"Boyfriend"	Me'Shell NdegéOcello	Me'Shell NdegéOcello	Urban/Hip Hop
Motown Collection	Motown Artists	James Jamerson	Classic R&B/Pop
"Long Walk"	Jill Scott	Don Stevens	Urban/R&B
Sportin' Life	Weather Report	Victor Bailey	Contemporary Jazz/ Jazz Fusion
Sgt. Pepper's Lonely Hearts Club Band, The White Album, etc.	The Beatles	Paul McCartney	Rock/Pop
Parliament Live	Parliament/Funkadelic	Bootsy Collins	Funk
Any Love	Luther Vandross	Marcus Miller	Contemporary R&B
Little Worlds	Bela Fleck and the Flecktones	Victor Wooten	Eclectic/jazz fusion/ world beat

3. Listen Actively

Here's roadblock number three on my list. Sometimes a song may appear to be very simple, so too little time is taken in learning it. I've had students in my classes make this mistake many times. When the tune was counted off, they would:

- completely forget the bass line.
- turn the phrasing of the bass line around by starting it on the wrong beat.
- play the bass line without any of the nuances that make it groove: staccato, legato, proper grouping of notes, correct syncopation, etc.
- make lots of mistakes.

I call the remedy for this **active listening**. If you are learning a song for an audition or to perform in a band, a good habit to get into is to learn the "whole" song. Learn the main melody and the parts of the other instruments, not just the bass line. This practice will allow you to become closer to the music by knowing and understanding its inner workings. Give yourself some time to really learn everything you can about the song.

Taking some time to learn a song does not mean you are not a good musician. Don't fall into the trap of this type of thinking. Take all the time you need. Imagine how it would feel if you hastily learned a simple-sounding song for an audition, only to make some of the above mistakes when it's your turn to perform. You won't get the gig, so don't let this happen to you!

I recommend using the following list to make sure you don't miss anything when learning new material.

Active Listening Checklist

1. Length of notes: legato, staccato, etc. Are some notes much longer or shorter than others? Are eighth-note rock lines played as sixteenth notes with sixteenth rests in between? Is there an uneven or full eighth-note feel?
2. Attack: is the line played with a light touch or an aggressive touch?
3. Straight or swing, and what degree of swing (heavily swung, light swing, etc.)?
4. Is the bass tone round and full, or top heavy, such as a slap bass tone?
5. Is the bass line a keyboard bass line?
6. Phrasing: are certain notes grouped together, heavier or lighter than others?
7. Are there lots of ghost notes? No ghost notes?
8. Does the bass line match the bass drum pattern?

Listening for these nuances is a skill that is developed over time. If you use this checklist often, it will eventually become second nature.

4. Listen to Yourself as You Play

The valuable skill of listening to oneself play is easier for some to develop than others. It is something that many players have never thought about, or that many players think they are doing but are not. There is a simple test to figure out if you're truly hearing yourself as you play: listen to earlier recordings of your performances in gigs and rehearsals. If you don't have any recordings of your performances, set up a recorder and tape your next rehearsal or gig in its entirety. Be very honest with yourself in your analysis of the recordings. Are you rushing or dragging consistently? If the answer is yes, then the skill of listening to yourself is not developed to its fullest potential. Once you have developed this skill, you will be able to remedy the problem of rushing or dragging with note placement as you are playing.

Listening as You Play Exercise

You'll need a tape or digital recorder for this exercise.

It requires you to develop and use a form of split focus—in this case, listening to another instrument as you play. Select a song that you are comfortable playing. Play the song five times, each time listening to a different instrument as you play along. Record each performance.

1. For the first recording, listen to the drums all the way through as you play along.
2. For the second recording, listen to the vocal or lead line all the way through as you play along.
3. For the third recording, listen to yourself playing all the way through.
4. For the fourth recording, scan different instruments as you play the different parts of the song, i.e., for the verse, listen to vocal or lead, then for the chorus, listen to the drums, then for the bridge, listen to yourself.
5. For the fifth recording, listen to yourself and the drums at the same time.

As you listen back to your performances, recall your thought process and the instrument(s) to which you were listening. Note how well you performed. Make note of any problems in your playing (by now you should be getting pretty good at this), and repeat the particular split focus exercise which gave you the most problem. This exercise will allow you the opportunity to concentrate on splitting your focus onto two or more functions at once. A split focus allows you to objectively listen to yourself playing so you can discern things like note placement, length of notes, phrasing, etc., as you play. With time, you will notice that in live situations, you are well able to listen to yourself as you play.

Groove Practice Exercise

For this exercise, re-use the recorded examples from the Listening/Analysis exercise to practice grooving. Learn the bass lines and then record yourself playing on a regular basis, recording and analyzing your performance to measure the progress of your playing.

Puddle of Mudd:	**Track 12** with bass–**Track 13** without bass
D'Angelo:	**Track 14** with bass–**Track 15** without bass
Jackson Five:	**Track 16** with bass–**Track 17** without bass
Parliament/Funkadelic:	**Track 18** with bass–**Track 19** without bass
Neo Soul:	**Track 20** with bass–**Track 21** without bass
Aerosmith:	**Track 22** with bass–**Track 23** without bass

 Technique

5

Good technique is a very important aspect of having a great groove. Bad technique can be the cause of groove killers such as too much string noise, buzzing, poor tone, shallow-sounding notes, undefined notes, missed notes, breakup of phrasing, and general sloppiness. Good technique comes from having great **tone**, **touch**, and **facility**.

Great Tone and Touch

Getting a nice round tone out of your bass, whether you are using fingerstyle or slapping technique, comes from your hands: your fingers should touch the fretboard in a strong, clean manner, allowing the best sound to come from your instrument. Of course the type and condition of the bass, amplifier, effects, and strings will all affect your tone, but ultimately you should have good technique to start. Nonetheless, it's a good idea to have a reputable luthier check out and set up your bass.

Facility

Your facility has to do with how well you get around on your instrument. The first element of facility is musical knowledge or theory. This plays a very large part in your groove because the better you are able to perform scales, modes, and patterns in all positions up and down the neck of your bass, the better you are able to play whatever is required without hesitation.

The other element of facility is your hand strength and stamina, finger dexterity, independence, and speed, collectively known by the slang term **chops**. Beginners and players who don't practice enough to keep their chops up may not be able to press the strings down hard or accurately enough to get a good, clear sound. This can also severely limit one's ability to execute many technically difficult bass lines.

Left Hand

The fretting hand fingers are slightly bent, spread out one-per-fret over four frets, and the thumb is placed on the back of the neck. Avoid gripping the neck like a baseball bat with your thumb wrapped around the neck and your palm touching the back.

Right Hand

Keep your wrist as straight as possible. Too much bend in your wrist can cause cramping when you are playing fast and/or hard, limit your facility, and cause damage to your hand. Most players keep the right thumb anchored on a pickup cover or installed thumb rest. This allows you to pluck with plenty of power and provides a stable reference point. Some players, however, prefer to keep the thumb off the instrument with a more free-floating hand posture that gives lots of freedom and facilitates a ready switch to a thumb-slapping position. Finally, some players use their thumb as a combination anchor and string damper for muting unwanted sound from the lower strings while playing the high ones. This technique allows for a very clean sound in the studio while sacrificing a little bit of string-striking power.

There are also many right-hand techniques for achieving various tones from your instrument, including plucking closer to or farther from the bridge, and using a plastic or felt pick. They are all legitimate and should be explored when you are ready and willing. For the purpose of grooving with a basic two- or three-finger playing style, pluck the strings near the front bass pickup (about halfway between the bridge and the end of the fingerboard) just below the tips of your fingers. To create the best possible sound, there is a balance you will want to achieve as your fingers roll off the strings. Let's call this perfect balance the "sweet spot."

Try the following methods of striking the string using different fingertip positioning and notice how the sound changes from position to position.

- Start on the very tip of your first finger and strike the string; notice the tone this produces.
- Start slightly lower on the tip of your first finger and strike the string; notice the tone this produces.
- Start lower, on the meaty part of your fingertip and strike the string; notice the tone this produces.

Experiment with this process and determine which position produces the best tone. Good positioning will produce a nice full, round tone.

Try to achieve a rolling motion in alternating your right-hand fingers, as opposed to a stabbing or yanking motion, as a normal part of playing the strings. Stabbing or yanking can cause an undesirable clicking string noise, resulting in a weak tone that is lacking in volume.

Once you find the best sounding finger-to-string placement or "sweet spot," strive to lock it into your memory and be consistent in using it.

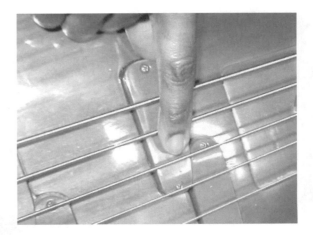

Building Chops

The more control you have over your chops, the better you will be able to execute bass lines with ease and confidence. Since this book is about groove and not specifically about building chops, I'll just provide enough exercises to get you started in the right direction.

Technique Exercise

Always make sure to warm up by playing something you already know very slowly before working on the following exercises (or anything new or challenging).

The object of this exercise is to apply the discussed technique points: a solid left-hand base, the right-hand sweet spot, a straight right wrist, and rolling finger motion, while performing the groove.

Start with your left-hand fingers correctly positioned in a solid base at the second fret.

Keep one finger per fret throughout the example except for those places where you play consecutive notes on the same fret but different strings. For the cleanest sound, I suggest not using the same finger twice in a row when changing from string to string. Practice the example using the fingering numbers below the notation; they illustrate this approach. After you feel comfortable playing the groove, record your performance.

Track 26 (with bass)

With a swing feel ♩ = 90

Listen back very closely to make sure you are getting a clean sound, and check for any of the above-mentioned problems. (Note: some string noise is natural.) If you hear enough noise, breaks in phrasing, time, etc., that the sound/feel of the groove is interfered with, technique adjustments should be made.

Adjustment Exercise

1. Isolate the part of the groove where you hear buzzing, shallow or missed notes, breaks in phrasing, or any of the other above-mentioned problems.

2. Keeping the same fingering and your hand in the same position as when you are playing the groove, press down on the fret of the problem note(s) harder and/or at different points within the fret. This may require shifting your wrist and/or forearm. You should hear clearer sounding notes at some point as you move your left hand and/or fingers around and strike the string. You may even notice that you have to press down harder on the fret to get the notes to sound clear. Note the adjustments that you have made in order to get the clearer note, smoother phrasing, or better note transition.

3. Now play the groove at a slower tempo, emphasizing the adjustments when you get to the trouble spots. You may notice fatigue after doing this several times. The fatigue is part of building strength. Again, make sure you have warmed up slowly, and stop if the fatigue sensation becomes one of pain.

4. Continue to play the groove at the slower tempo until you can perform it in time and without any problems, then speed up the tempo in increments of three beats per minute, until you surpass the original tempo by ten beats per minute.

If you are having problems, please do not skip the above four steps. You will only be prolonging your journey to the groove. By repeating these steps, you are isolating problem areas with your left-hand strength and dexterity. Continue to use this process on other grooves. When you are able to perform the grooves with a good clean sound and without fatigue, you are benefiting from your solid left-hand base and building your chops.

The internet is a great resource for finding technique exercises, tips, and lessons. Since web sites and their addresses come and go so quickly, rather than list them in this book, the best I can do is suggest that you type "bass guitar lessons" or a similar phrase into a search engine such as Yahoo or Google, and be prepared for a tidal wave of results. Also, please check my web site at www.groovemastery.com for further technique help.

Practicing

6

Of course practicing is obvious and necessary. Here are some tips for practicing which I have found to be useful. Try to practice a few hours every day. I suggest no less than three hours, but more would be even better if you can swing it. The late, great Jaco Pastorius spoke of practicing nine hours a day in his *Modern Electric Bass* video. Though the following suggestions are designed to coincide with improving your groove, you should also practice scales, arpeggios, modes, and reading, as these are things that will make you a more complete player.

Tip 1: Practice with a Metronome

Always practice with a metronome. Playing with a drum machine is also okay, but, as stated in the introduction, they will not give you a true representation of your own feel and time. This is because you hear the momentum of the drum machine carrying you along as opposed to hearing the momentum of your own playing. When you first learn an exercise or groove, start practicing it at slower speeds, i.e., 60 to 65 bpm. Practicing slowly is VERY important in developing your groove. The tendency is to practice at whatever tempo is comfortable: usually medium to fast tempos. The problem here is that you don't gain control over your playing. When performing a more difficult bass line you may slow down or gloss over the line. Some lines or exercises are actually more difficult to execute at a much slower tempo. When you rely on momentum to get you through, slower grooves are difficult because you don't have complete control of your playing. Relying on momentum would be great if the only tempos that you were required to play were tempos that you were already comfortable playing.

Tip 2: Set the Metronome on Two and Four

Set the metronome to half the original tempo of a song, and then start saying, "two... four" along with the clicks. When you've got that going, then add the words "one" and "three" in between. Now the metronome is only giving you the backbeat (the part usually played by the snare drum), instead of clicking all the quarter or eighth notes. Playing along with the metronome set like this will aid in developing your own sense of time. Now you can't depend on hearing the downbeat, and so you are working on feeling it on your own (sounds easy, but it's really not).

Tip 3: Practice Playing Along with CDs, Tapes, and Radio

This is a great escape from the usual metronome practice and the feeling of playing in isolation. It also helps to keep things interesting, stimulates creativity, and develops a feel for playing in live situations.

Tip 4: Put Together a Practice Band

Though it may be a hassle to put together a practice band, the payoff will be well worth it. It will help you make the transition from practicing alone with a metronome in your living room to playing with live musicians. Live playing chops and practice chops are very different. Practicing at home with a metronome is usually calm and controlled—without the pressures of having to play accurately through songs and sets nonstop, while live playing increases your energy and excitement level. This can cause you to abandon your technique by playing too hard, stiffening your fingers and wrists. Pain, fatigue, and difficulty executing bass lines can result. Since you will have to call upon more of yourself mentally and physically when playing live, it's important to build your live playing chops. A balance of practicing at home and playing live is important. Using a practice band will make this transition easier.

Chapter 6

Tip 5: Record Yourself Often

Recording your performances both in live and practice situations is an invaluable tool in measuring progress in playing. Keep track of the recordings and periodically listen to older performances. This process not only enables you to assess your progress, it will also help hone the skill of identifying incremental time shifts. The more you use this skill, the more adept you will become.

Tip 6: Surround Yourself with Good Musicians

Go to musician hangs, mingle, make connections, and solicit lessons from players you admire. Many of the players you hear on your favorite recordings are willing to teach. Find playing situations with good musicians who are better than you are. All these things will help you to become a better musician.

Tip 7: Practice with the Correct Strap Adjustment

The position of your instrument is very important. First, make sure your bass is not hanging too low just because you think it looks cool. This positioning will cause too much bend in your left wrist and wreak havoc on your technique. On the other hand, positioning the bass too high will cause too much bend in your right wrist. Find a balance where there is not too much bend in either wrist. Second, adjust your strap so that you practice with your bass in the same position sitting and standing. Otherwise your technique will be completely thrown off if you practice sitting down, and play live standing up.

Anti-Groove Don'ts from the Groove Police

Often there's not much time to think when you're on a gig, so this obnoxious list is here to give you things to consider while practicing. Keep in mind that you are training your reflexes, and the way you practice is the way you will wind up playing live.

PLEASE DON'T:

- rush or drag the tempo.
- play stiff or mechanically.
- play without conviction. If you're not sure what the right part is, find out.
- overplay.
- play without listening to others in the band.
- play without definition (i.e., too light of a touch, glossing over the top, not digging in).
- lose your focus and/or concentration and make lots of mistakes.
- play the wrong feel or style: jazz licks in a pop tune, etc.
- fake chops you don't have.
- ignore ugly tone, buzzing, or string noise.
- play out of tune.
- use lazy or nonexistent string damping (causing strings not being played to ring out over the bass line).
- make excuses for lame playing.

What can I say... try not to get arrested for any of these violations.

Phrasing

7

Notes are grouped together to form short musical thoughts. These are phrases. If you play all the correct notes but it still feels like something is missing, it's possible you are not aware of where one phrase ends and another one begins. You should phrase a bass line to follow or support the phrases played by the rest of the band. You could say, at its very simplest, supportive phrasing is accomplished by clearly playing the root of a chord on the downbeat at the beginning of a phrase, thus helping all the other musicians keep their places. In actual practice, the arrangement and length of **all** the notes and rests contributes to correct phrasing, as do the placement of accents, legato or staccato notes, ghost notes, grace notes, and slurs.

I think of phrasing as the blueprint or essential identity of a bass line. You should memorize the phrasing as a part of learning someone else's music. In writing your own music and your own bass lines, it is obviously very valuable to understand phrasing in order to create the best groove for a particular piece of music.

Phrase Lengths

Awareness of the beginning and end of each two-, four-, or eight-bar phrase is necessary to be in control and maintain a solid groove. This is of the highest importance, as is the awareness of phrasing in long vamps where another instrument is soloing. You will need to be aware of the end of eight, twelve, sixteen, or even more bars in order to anticipate and build with the music as well as the ends of solos. Some sections are phrased with an irregular number of bars, which you should also try to support with your playing. Very often different instruments play phrases of different lengths at the same time that encompass or even overlap each other, adding to the intricacy of the music. An example of this is an eight-bar melody over a two-bar groove played four times. Awareness of this type of compositional structure will help you advance as a player.

The way to go about acquiring such musicianship is by counting bars as you play. This should be done until it becomes ingrained at a subconscious level, so that if someone were to stop you at any time, you could tell him/her that you were on beat two of measure three, for instance, when the music stopped.

Phrase Length Exercise

Track 12 (with bass)

Track 13 (without bass)

Track 12 ("Blurry"), with which you may be familiar by now, consists of a repeated four-measure phrase. Count the **measure numbers and the quarter-note beats** aloud while listening to this track.

"**One** two three four, **Two** two three four, **Three** two three four, **Four** two three four..."

Practice counting aloud like this for the duration of the track, listening to how the phrase fits into the four-bar space. If you're not used to it, counting steadily is harder than you might think. Do it again, this time while playing to Track 13, but only playing as much of the bass line as you can manage while still counting. For the purpose of learning to count the phrases, you can have as many mistakes or dropped notes in the bass line as necessary, but do not stop counting for any reason (except to breathe!). Make counting bars and beats the priority for now.

Track 14 (with bass)

Track 15 (without bass)

Track 14 ("D'Angelo") consists of two-bar phrases. Repeat the process of counting bars and beats aloud while playing along with Track 15.

Track 16 (with bass)

Track 17 (without bass)

"Jackson Five": count four-bar phrases.

Track 18 (with bass)

Track 19 (without bass)

"Parliament/Funkadelic": count four-bar phrases.

Track 20 (with bass)

Track 21 (without bass)

"Neo Soul": While the bass part for the verses is a two-bar phrase, you should count eight-bar phrases for these verse sections. The chorus requires you to count a six-bar phrase.

Track 22 (with bass)

Track 23 (without bass)

"Aerosmith": Count eight measures while the two-bar intro riff is played four times, then count a sixteen-measure verse, then an eight-bar chorus.

"Go for It Well" on Fills or Licks

A crucial element of strong phrasing is knowing when to stick to the established bass line and when to play a fill or lick. Inappropriately placed or excessive licks or fills (such as every four bars) can be real groove killers. The situation may require that you get only one chance to step out and play a lick, so choose your moment and "go for it well." Here's what I mean by this...

- Make sure you're not stepping on any toes, i.e., clashing with the vocal or melodic lead.

- Make sure you know what lick you're going to play before you attempt it. There are several implications here. You can get caught up in letting your fingers and muscle memory lead you. This may end up sounding okay, but after listening to a large number of my students over many years, I can say with certainty that it usually creates an amateurish, noodling sound. To avoid sounding this way, build an arsenal of licks (listening to other bass players and coming up with some of your own) and practice playing them in all keys and at slow and fast tempos, so that you know exactly how they'll sound when you apply them.

- Simple as it sounds, play your lick in time. Since you are straying from the bass line, it is very easy to drag the tempo if you're playing a lick with lots of notes. If you're slapping a lick, it is common to rush the tempo. Also, it's very common to miss the downbeat of the next phrase (not good!).

- Use your lick to set up the downbeat of the next bar of music, or in other words, set up "one." One of the biggest parts of grooving is setting up the downbeat of the next phrase so that the listener and everyone in the band can feel exactly where it is. A great groover is proficient and consistent with this.

- Make sure your lick is appropriate to the musical piece. There are always those times and opportunities to use your chops and play fast fancy licks, but when you are interested in going for it well while staying in the groove, doing the right thing may mean playing less.

- Study the rhythms of drum fills of popular drummers in each of the genres. Note how the rhythms of the fills flow, and use these rhythms to create some of your own licks. Also, note the rhythms of fills of drummers you are currently playing with and experiment with playing fills that match their rhythms. This is a very powerful technique which allows you get away from the bass line and still stay very much in the groove, because you are still locked in with the drummer.

- Take cues from the lead or melodic instruments by playing the melody with them at the beginning or end of a bass line.

Chapter 7

Protecting Your Groove

Be a thinking bass player and **care for every note**.

In protecting your groove by caring for every note, you must be focused. Some common considerations: if you should use a harder or softer attack, if the note is too long or too short, if you should emphasize this beat or that beat, if you should play a two-bar fill or four-bar fill, if you should stick to the bass line, what is coming up in the next section of the song, what tone you are producing from a particular technique, if you should lay back or push the drummer's feel, and on and on.

This sounds like too much to think about, but actually, when you become a polished player with a great groove, you are doing all of these things and more—you may add singing background or even lead vocals, and/or dancing and jumping around—or as in Victor Wooten's case, throwing the bass around your shoulders in the middle of a solo and not missing a beat! Well, yeah, that is a lot to think about, but it just goes to show that we are capable of multi-tasking as musicians, and it's amazing how many things we can process at once. They become second nature after working long and hard, applying all of your studies. Some of these concepts may be difficult at first, but as you become increasingly aware of these details and practice each one, they will become reflexes rather than conscious thoughts.

Not being a thinking bass player and not protecting your groove can make your playing sound too light and "fluffy," like it's glossing **over the top** of the groove instead of being **down in it.** If anyone ever tells you your groove is "fluffy," you know you're in bad shape.

Three big offenders of not protecting your groove are **cheating a note, throwing away the end of a phrase**, and **changing the syncopation** of a phrase.

Cheating Notes

Track 24 (full-value notes)

Track 25 (cheated notes)

Cheating a note happens when you chop the note too short so that the full time value is not played. If you transcribe a bass line that has quarter notes and play them as eighth notes instead, you are cheating the notes. The sound of the bass line with the quarter notes is more legato but your interpretation has a staccato sound, creating a stiff, unbalanced groove. Listen to Track 24 (full value notes), then listen to Track 25 (cheated notes). Compare the sound and feel of the full-value groove as opposed to the cheated-note groove and you'll hear a definite difference between the two.

The important thing to take from this is that if you are recording for a producer or playing for an artist, they know how their music should feel. If the groove is out of balance due to cheated notes, they may not be able to state the exact problem, but will know something is wrong. The finger is pointed at you, and you will need to know how to rectify it. The problem of cheating a note goes back to listening closely to yourself play. Make sure you listen for the nuances of the bass line—including the correct note lengths—and incorporate them.

Throwing Away the End of a Phrase

An example of this can be when you are playing the verse of a song while thinking ahead to the chorus. The notes at the end of the verse phrase are played in a rushed, careless manner because you stopped thinking about what you were playing at the moment. This problem has to do with note placement and listening to yourself. The remedy will have to come with the realization that this is indeed a problem in your playing. Go back and listen to previous recordings of your live performances and look for this particular issue. If you find you are throwing away the ends of phrases, it can be remedied by the practice of splitting your focus: thinking about note placement and thinking forward to the next section of the song at the same time. This is another aspect of becoming a thinking bass player.

Changing the Syncopation of a Phrase

Just as it sounds, this happens when you misinterpret bass lines by moving notes that belong on upbeats to downbeats, or vice versa, in your interpretation. It can be the result of not listening closely enough when you're learning a bass line, or from having difficulty playing certain syncopated combinations.

These are all very common groove errors which can be fixed if you are honest in your self-diagnosis and thorough in your efforts to apply the cures. It's all in the process of protecting your groove, being a thinking bass player, and caring for every note.

8 Straight Feel and Swing Feel

Every good musician should know the difference between a swing feel and a straight feel. Each is more predominant in certain styles of music, which is even more support for the argument that you should expose yourself to many genres. It takes work and practice to learn to make a convincing switch from a straight feel to a swing feel and back again.

Since swing is an interpretation of music, musicians do not learn it as beginners. Swing is basically concerned with the exact timing of when upbeat notes are attacked. However, your interpretation of accents, legatos, and staccatos as well as how you slur and tie the notes will also have an effect on making a particular tune swing the way it should.

Basic Eighth-Note Feels

Straight eighth notes are even subdivisions of quarter notes. In a straight eighth-note feel, notes starting on downbeats and upbeats are of the same duration. The sound of straight eighth notes is even and mechanical, like a ticking clock.

At slow to medium tempos, eighth notes played with a swing feel are basically equivalent to eighth-note triplets with the middle note removed. Compared to straight eighth notes, the notes on the upbeats are now played later and so must be of shorter duration. Notes on downbeats are consequently of longer duration. Rather than sounding mechanical, swing feels sound more human and "bouncy" or flowing. To experience the slow-tempo swing feel, also known as a **shuffle**, count even triplets aloud like this: "one two three, one two three, one two three, one two three." Now repeat the quotation, but snap your mouth shut instead of saying "two" each time. That's a basic shuffle or slow swing feel.

The equivalence to triplet subdivision does not apply to eighth-note swing feels at faster tempos. As tempos increase, the difference in duration and attack time between upbeat and downbeat notes diminishes until at very high tempos, swing feels are nearly indistinguishable from straight feels. Therefore, at faster tempos, a true swing feel is somewhere in between a triplet feel and a straight-eighth feel, becoming straighter as the tempo increases. This is all only an explanation of swing in the most basic sense. There are myriad variations in accents, note lengths, and the degree of temporal displacement of upbeat notes that you could read about forever and not really "feel," but are fairly easily understood by hearing and imitating.

As bassists concerned with the intricacies of groove, next we're going to look at straight and swing feels at the sixteenth-note subdivision level.

Straight-Sixteenth Feel

In a straight-sixteenth feel, quarter notes are evenly divided into four sixteenth notes of equal length, whether they are all played or some are merely implied. The syncopation examples we studied in Chapter One all had a straight-sixteenth feel. We counted it like this: "1 e and a, 2 e and a, 3 e and a, 4 e and a," with each note being the same duration as the others. On Track 27, you'll hear straight sixteenth notes played on one pitch, with the metronome at 90 bpm.

Track 27

Though the straight feel is easily recognizable and easier to play, there are those who have worked more with swing feel and have difficulty playing feels with straight sixteenths. Traditionally, classic and modern rock, heavy metal, speed metal, pop, some funk, and R&B require that you have a very strong grasp of the straight feel, though the lines between straight to swing are occasionally crossed in these genres. Track 28 is a typical groove with a straight-sixteenth feel.

Track 28

Swing-Sixteenth Feel

In a swing-sixteenths feel, the upbeats—the "e's" and "a's"—happen later, making them shorter than the downbeat notes. The sixteenth subdivisions of the quarter note are played or felt in an uneven long–short–long–short pattern, as follows:

1	–	(1st 16th) –	long
e	–	(2nd 16th) –	short and closer to the next sixteenth downbeat
and	–	(3rd 16th) –	long
a	–	(4th 16th) –	short and closer to the next sixteenth downbeat

The swing feel can come from the hi-hat, ghost notes played by the snare, the kick drum, guitar, bass, etc.—any rhythm instrument playing sixteenth notes. For our purposes, the swing will come from the sixteenth notes within the bass line. You'll hear swing sixteenths played on one pitch with a metronome at 70 bpm on Track 29.

Track 29

Swing charts are notated as straight sixteenths with the instruction "with a swing feel" over the first measure of music. A good groover turns that notation into the swing feel without thinking too much about it.

Swing feel must be understood and mastered in order to play hip-hop, contemporary and classic/old school R&B, pop, funk, reggae, contemporary jazz, smooth jazz, and many other styles. If you plan to be a well-rounded musician and you haven't worked much with the swing feel, it is a good idea to spend lots of time on it.

Track 30

Listen to Track 30, which is a groove played with a swing feel. Go back to the straight sixteenth groove, Track 28, and compare it with the feel of the swinging sixteenth groove. Note the difference between the two feels. Though there are a number of differences, you can feel that the swinging groove is more round sounding, whereas the straight groove is more squared off.

Swing in Different Degrees

A further factor of difficulty in playing the swing feel is that it can be played in a more or less exaggerated way. The amount of swing you'll use depends on the music you're playing. In the following visual demonstration, I used a midi sequencing program that allows you to quantize the swing feel by degree. I programmed a midi bass line using four different degrees of swing. These are screenshots of the actual recordings, so you can see and hear the difference in the amount of swing in the examples. The notes which give the swing feel are circled, so you can see how they are moved to create different swing feels.

0% swing groove is a straight feel. Notice how the sixteenth notes (the short dashes) are the same length. The beats are evenly divided.

Track 31

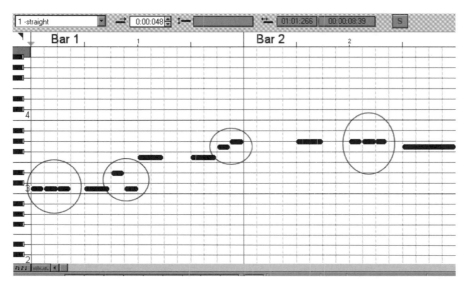

Now look at an 87% swing groove. Notice how the sixteenths starting on upbeats have shortened and shifted slightly.

Track 32

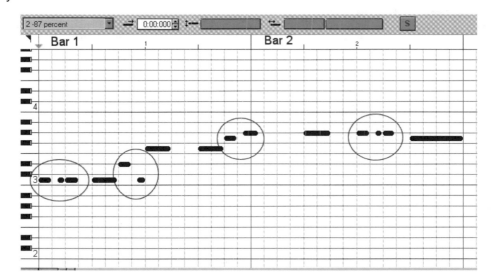

67% swing groove. Notice how the sixteenths have shortened and/or shifted slightly.

Track 33

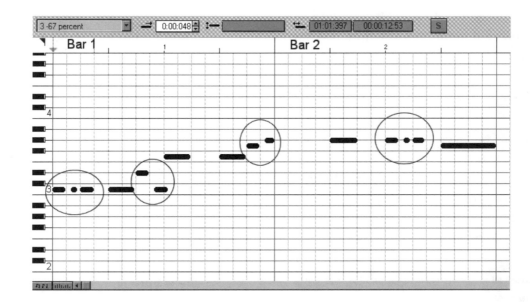

59% swing groove. Again, the sixteenths have shortened and/or shifted slightly.

Track 34

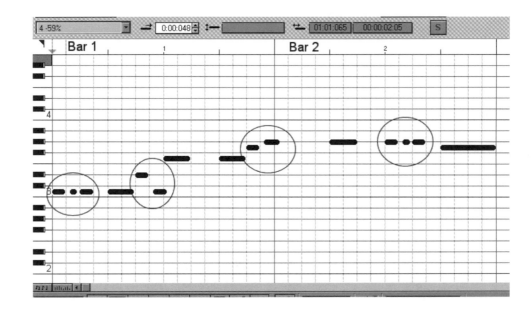

When you listen to these midi grooves one after the other, you will notice that the less swing, the more relaxed the groove sounds. How much swing you should use depends on the music and the composer's intentions. It's important that all the players agree and use the same amount, in most cases.

Straight to Swing Feel Exercise

In the following exercise, you will be playing the same groove, both in straight-sixteenth feel and in swing feel. Remember that the notation for straight and swing feel is the same, but that swing feel is indicated as "with a swing feel" notated on the music. Both the bass and drum tracks are recorded in both feels.

Listen to the straight feel of the groove on Track 35, then play along with the drum track, Track 37. The groove is relatively simple to play so that the emphasis is put into making the switch from straight feel to swing feel.

Track 35 (with bass)   Track 37 (without bass)

Straight Groove

Now, listen very carefully to the swing groove, Track 36. Notice the "long–short–long–short" sixteenth-note feel. Then, play along with the drum track, Track 38.

Track 36 (with bass)   Track 38 (without bass)

Swing Groove

With a swing feel

Swing Listening

It may take some time to get comfortable playing the swing feel. Plan on spending some time with it and you will notice improvement. Also listening to music that is swung is an absolute must in order to get this feel in your heart and under your fingers. With that in mind, here is a partial listening list. As with the other lists, it's a place to start, so continue to add to it and make it your own as you hear songs that you identify as having a swing feel.

Song or CD Title	Artist
"No Scrubs"	TLC
"I'm So Into You"	SWV
Play Date	Euge Groove
Tender Lover	Babyface
Niice N' Wild	Chuckii Booker
Smooth	Gerald Albright
Don't Be Cruel, "On My Own"	Bobby Brown
Still Small Voice	Paul Jackson Jr.
"No Diggity"	Black Street
"Virtual Insanity"	Jamiroquai
"On and On"	Erykah Badu
"She Came in Through the Bathroom Window"	Joe Cocker
"Rebirth of Slick (Cool Like Dat)"	Digable Planets
Sledge Hammer	Peter Gabriel
Jus Chillin'	Norman Brown
"Pick Up the Pieces"	Candi Dulfer
Let It Ripp	The Rippingtons
Voodoo, "Shit, Damn, M.F."	D'Angelo
P-Funk (Wants to Get Funked Up)	Parliament/Funkadelic
"Intro," *Live and More*	Marcus Miller
"Video"	India Arie

Ghost Notes

9

Track 39

A ghost note is a small percussive muted note which has no pitch associated with it. Listen to Track 39 for an example of ghost notes mixed in with regular, full-value notes. Ghost notes can add an expressive rhythmic dimension to your playing, but whenever a layer of complexity is added to anything, the potential for problems increases. Let's look at some common problems associated with the use of ghost notes, along with some exercises to help fix them and build your ghost-note chops.

Incorrect Muting Technique

Ghost notes must be adequately muted to prevent a musical pitch from popping out instead of the desired percussive sound. This happens from lack of practice and/or experience with ghost notes. Here is an exercise to help your ghost notes sound solid and strong, yet without pitch.

Ghost Note Exercise 1

Play a full-value G quarter note on your E string using your left-hand second finger. Notice that to play the note and get a full round sound, you must use medium to heavy pressure. Now, lift your left-hand second finger very slightly off the string so that you are not using as much pressure. Strike the G again, this time using the very tip of your right-hand finger and using more force. (This is a muted plucking technique that creates a ghost note.) This should produce a nice strong ghost note. Go back and forth between playing a full G note and a G ghost note. Notice the changes needed in both your right and left hands to make a definite difference in the two sounds.

Now try the same exercise using various notes in different positions. Notice that the amount of left-hand finger pressure required to play ghost notes as well as normal notes varies as you move about the neck. Also, playing ghost notes at the nodal points of the strings (for instance, the fifth fret of each string) on your bass can cause an unintended harmonic overtone to be produced. Experiment with moving your right hand around and muting with more than one finger in the left hand so that a harmonic tone is not produced.

In the next exercise you will use all four of your fretting fingers to produce a full-value note, then a ghost note. Start with your left hand at the first fret on the fourth string of your bass.

Ghost Note Exercise 2

Ghost notes are notated by an "x" on the staff. If you accidentally produce a live pitch instead of a completely dead ghost note, you'll want it to be a note that fits the music, so the ghost note is written on the note where your finger should be on the staff. Using eighth notes and starting at 80 bpm, play this exercise using the left-hand fingering shown below the written notation. It's one finger per fret, all the way up and down the strings in first position.

Track 40

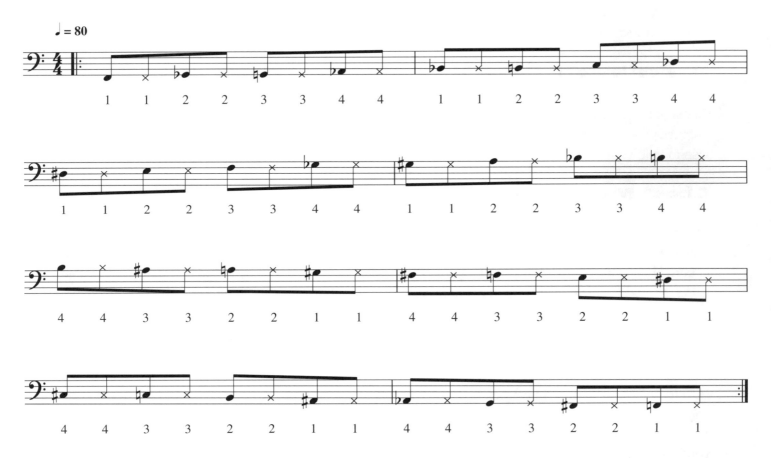

Start this exercise at the suggested tempo for ten minutes (it will feel like an eternity but try to stick with it). Move up in tempo by increments of five beats per minute until you reach 160 bpm. Once you have done this for a few months, continue to play at faster tempos on a daily basis to build chops. You will find that playing ghost notes requires lots of hand strength, and this will make you a stronger player.

Swinging Ghost Notes

I remember one student in particular who was an amazing bassist with natural talent. He could easily execute difficult bass lines using ghost notes in straight feel, but he could not make the switch to swinging the ghost notes, which is often necessary to give a bass line the swing feel. He knew something was wrong, but he could not identify that he was playing his ghost notes with a straight-sixteenth feel. After I pointed this out to him, he began to work on making his ghost notes swing. Even though he was a very good musician, it needed to be pointed out that his ghost note usage in swing feel was lacking and causing problems with his groove.

Ghost Note Exercise 3

Set your metronome to quarter notes only. This way, you can switch back and forth between the swing feel and straight feel without stopping. I recommend starting this exercise at 68 bpm. It's a deliberately slow tempo, and this is the best way to gain control of your ghost notes if you have not had much experience. (If you have more experience with ghost notes, start at a higher tempo, say 95 bpm, and go higher from there.) Use full-value sixteenth notes and ghost notes, and alternate between straight feel and swing feel. Once you make a distinct difference between the two feels, you can begin to increase the tempo.

Track 39 (with swing feel)

Track 41 (with straight feel)

Ghost Note Exercise 4

The next exercise is played in straight-sixteenth feel. As you listen, notice how the ghost notes are spaced evenly before the following downbeat. As you perform the exercise, strive to play solid, consistent ghost notes, making sure they land in time. The exercise is recorded at 85 bpm, but you should start playing it at a slower tempo if necessary, allowing you to gain control of your playing by feeling the space in between the notes. Practicing this on a daily basis will help with awareness of rushing, dragging, and overall feel for time. As in the previous exercise, use a metronome as opposed to a drum machine, and set it to play quarter notes.

Track 42

Overuse of Ghost Notes

Too much of a good thing can be a problem. To decide if you play too many ghost notes, listen to your interpretation of bass lines from past performances. If you change the original bass line drastically, adding lots of ghost notes and/or change full-value notes into ghost notes, you are playing too many ghost notes. If this is the case, it could imply that you are not listening to a wide variety of music and/or bass players. The amount of ghost notes you use should depend on the genre of music and/or song you are playing. Playing too many ghost notes tends to imply fusion-ish or jazzy playing. This is fine if you are playing contemporary jazz or fusion, but if you are playing more mainstream music, excessive ghost notes are simply not appropriate. The well-rounded player should be able to slip from one genre to the next seamlessly—and that means playing less (ghost notes or notes) when necessary.

Ghost Note Demons

There are a couple of other problems with ghost notes to be aware of. A big one is interpreting what should be a full-value note as a ghost note, or vice versa: interpreting a ghost note as a full-value note. Usually this happens as a result of insufficient listening to the original bass line and/or the genre it comes from. Misinterpreting ghost notes in this way can completely change the balance of a bass line, making for an amateurish-sounding groove. Another common mistake is to leave out ghost notes altogether, possibly because you didn't notice them, or just underestimated their importance to the groove.

Song Analysis

Below are seven songs with bass lines containing interesting usage of ghost notes. Once you have found recordings of these songs (if you use the internet, please download the songs from a legal site), transcribe and analyze them closely, as the ghost note usage is very different in each. Using the chart below, write in the characteristics of the ghost note usage: how many, how few, how they are used from one genre to the next, in what section of the song they are used, whether the beginning of the bass line is clean or ghosted, etc. You can also analyze ghost note usage in your favorite songs, but make sure that the genres are diverse. Analyzing the ghost notes in songs will help you to develop your instincts for when, where, and how to use them.

Ghost Note Analysis Song List

Song Title	Artist
"A Long Walk"	Jill Scott
"Sexy M.F."	Prince
"Big Pay Back" "Sex Machine"	James Brown
"Smooth"	D'Angelo
"Soul with a Capital S"	Tower of Power
"Low Rider"	War

I'll start you off by noting some characteristics in the first song. Try to think of others, and continue with the rest of the songs.

Ghost Note Analysis Chart

Song	Characteristic 1	Characteristic 2	Characteristic 3	Characteristic 4
"A Long Walk"	Ghost notes are used to create the swing feel.	Sparse usage in first verse, then usage increases to heavy as bass ad libs increase.	The beginning of the two-bar phrase never has a ghost note— always a clean downbeat. But the downbeat of the second bar of the two-bar phrase sometimes has a ghost note.	
"Sexy M.F."				
"Big Pay Back"				
"Sex Machine"				

Song	Characteristic 1	Characteristic 2	Characteristic 3	Characteristic 4
"Smooth"				
"Soul with a Capital S"				
"Low Rider"				

Ghost Note Exercise 5

Once you have transcribed and analyzed the above songs, record yourself playing each bass line with a metronome only, so you can accurately critique your performance. Then record yourself playing along with the original song. Use this process on a daily basis for each song until all are very easy and natural to play, both with a metronome and with the recording. You'll notice an obvious difference in your ghost note accuracy and your playing in general after doing this exercise on a regular basis.

10 Make It More Interesting

Innovators of the bass guitar such as Marcus Miller, James Jamerson, Bootsy Collins, Larry Graham, Jaco Pastorius, Paul McCartney, Lee Sklar, Nathan East, Ray Brown, Abe Laboriel (the list goes on and on) have shown us through their melodic, funky styles and amazing talents that bass playing is not just about holding the root and playing the fifth and octave. These players have elevated the importance of what used to be just a supporting instrument, and added a real sense of excitement and presence to the whole bass guitar gig, while blazing a trail for those coming after them to learn and grow.

When I began studying the bass, I was very much attracted to the different styles of playing, but I became even more interested when I heard those special little touches: that sweet low tone, with the addition of vibrato with just the right touch in just the right place; slap and pluck with that funky sparkle; double stops and harmonics to add melodic elegance, that's what I wanted to play. Being a self-taught player, I learned everything backwards because I got into all the flashy tricks before I really learned the basics. Needless to say, I had to go back to the very beginning and work on the fundamentals. I hope that this book will keep you from making the mistakes that I made.

As this book is about grooving and not the execution of special techniques, I won't describe each in detail. Instead I want you to focus your attention on determining the appropriate time and place to use them to contribute to the groove. I have started with several questions for each of these techniques that you should answer. You may be able to ask the same questions for the other techniques and come up with some questions of your own. After you listen to the examples, go to the "Make It More Interesting" chart to find bass players and songs associated with each technique. Find the recordings and analyze them with similar questions. Also try to intelligently analyze the use of special techniques in other songs with which you are familiar.

Vibrato

Track 43

Does this add or take away from the bass line?
Where is the vibrato used in the bass line: middle of phrase, end of phrase, on every note, etc.?
Does it affect the balance of the bass line in a good or bad way?

Grace Notes

Track 44

Do these add or take away from the bass line?
Where are the grace notes used in the bass line: middle of phrase, end of phrase, on every note, etc.?
Does it affect the balance of the bass line in a good or bad way?

Double Stops

Track 45

Is the double stop a part of the bass line or is used to punctuate the end of a phrase?
How does the double stop affect the flow of the bass line?

Harmonics

Track 46

Can you hear the harmonic clearly through all of the other parts in the music?

How does the harmonic affect the song?

How does the harmonic affect the bass line?

If you had performed this song, would you have used more harmonics? Less?

Bass Beat Box

Track 47

Did this technique inspire you? How did it inspire you?

Can you incorporate this technique into any of songs you currently perform?

If you were playing this song, would you use this technique more, or less? Why?

Can you think of other songs you have played or recorded in which this technique would be appropriate? Why?

Can you think of songs you have played or recorded in which this technique would not be appropriate? Why?

When considering the use of one of these techniques it's more important than ever to think of how your part fits into the overall performance of the song. Try to be objective in deciding when to play a little more, when to play less, and when to really step out.

"Make It More Interesting" Bass Player/Song List

Technique	Bassist	Song Title	Artist
Vibrato, Trills	Me'Shell NdegéOcello	"Boyfriend," "Plantation Lullabies"	Me'Shell NdegéOcello
	Abe Laboriel	"Memory Lane"	Minnie Ripperton
Grace Notes	Louis Johnson	"I Can't Help It," "Off the Wall"	Michael Jackson
Ghost Notes	Neil Stubenhaus	"Stay Home Tonight" "Sexy MF"	Lalah Hathaway Prince
Double Stops	Chuck Rainey	"Josie," "Peg," "Aja," "Along Came Betty"	Steely Dan Quincy Jones
	Pino Palladino	"Playa Playa," "Voodoo"	D'Angelo
Harmonics	Jimmy Haslip		Yellowjackets
	Deon Estus	"Heaven Help Me"	George Michael
Bass Beat Box	Marcus Miller	"Teen Town"	Marcus Miller

Closing

Congratulations! The fact that you purchased and worked with this book says that you are a serious musician. I am proud of you for the taking this step in making your dreams come true. Now that you have finished, go back to the beginning and do it all again! Revisit the chapters you feel you need to continue working with.

Becoming a seasoned groover takes lots of hard work and determination. At times you will want to say, "forget it" and chuck it all. Just know that this happens to most musicians, and that soon your passion for music will come back to you, and next thing you know you'll be back on track. Believe me, the satisfaction you will receive when you are on stage creating, playing, emoting, **grooving**, will make you happy you stayed with it. It's very hard to describe the rewards—and they are limitless—so keep working on it.

Bass players have come against some serious competition over the years with the advent of keyboard bass, samplers, ProTools, and the economics of the music business. Some artists and producers have been willing to sacrifice real bass guitar for keyboard bass. However, talent, creativity, feel, and let's face it, the plain ol' need to have the real players lay down some solid, funky grooving has kept the electric bass guitar an integral part of live and recorded music and has kept bass players working through some very rough times. On top of that, the organic sound of real instruments as opposed to machines has become "cool" again—good news for bass players—but you'd better be groovin'! So it's up to you as an up-and-coming bass player to take the torch and keep the bass guitar and bass playing in the forefront of music, and keep the groove alive!

I hope working with this book has been a rewarding experience. I wish you the best in your career as a bass player, and when your time comes, I look forward to hearing your contributions to and interpretation of the Groove.